BIG ANIMALS

by Anne Priestley
illustrated by Ian Jackson

Random House

Library of Congress Cataloging-in-Publication Data:
Priestley, Anne. Big animals. (Look and learn)
Includes index.
SUMMARY: Describes the physical characteristics, habits, and natural environment of twelve large mammals including the African elephant, polar bear, Indian tiger, and moose.   1. Mammals—Juvenile literature.
2. Mammals—Size—Juvenile literature.   [1. Mammals]
I. Jackson, Ian, 1960 — ill.   II. Title.   III. Series.
QL706.2.P75   1987   599   87-4621
ISBN: 0-394-89188-0 (trade); 0-394-99188-5 (lib. bdg.)

Phototypeset by Southern Positives and Negatives (SPAN), Lingfield, Surrey
Manufactured in Spain 1 2 3 4 5 6 7 8 9 0

Contents

The animals in this book are all mammals. Mammals are a group of animals. All mammals drink milk when they are babies and have hair or fur on their bodies. Dogs, cats, hamsters, and rabbits are mammals. Elephants and giraffes are mammals. So are people.

There are more than eight hundred thousand kinds of insects in the world and more than thirty thousand kinds of fishes. But there are only five thousand kinds of mammals.

4

Most mammals are smaller than people. Only a few kinds are really big. Big animals need so much food that they cannot live in fields or gardens. They can find enough food to eat only in much bigger places like grasslands and jungles.

This is a map of the world which shows where the animals in this book live. Most of them live in Africa, where there is plenty of wild open space.

Other countries in the world do not have so many big animals because people have taken over the wild places. They have built houses and farms and cut down the trees.

In these countries big animals can live only in the places where people do not want to live. Tigers live in the jungle. Polar bears, moose, and elephant seals live where it is very cold. Camels live in deserts where it is very dry. Bison live in huge parks which are kept wild just for them. And blue whales live in the vast oceans.

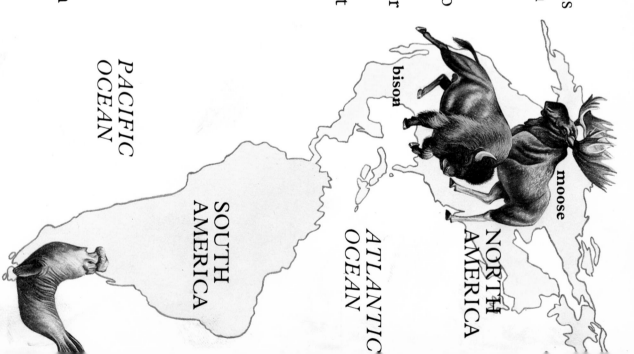

PACIFIC
OCEAN

SOUTH
AMERICA

bison

moose

NORTH
AMERICA

ATLANTIC
OCEAN

elephant seal

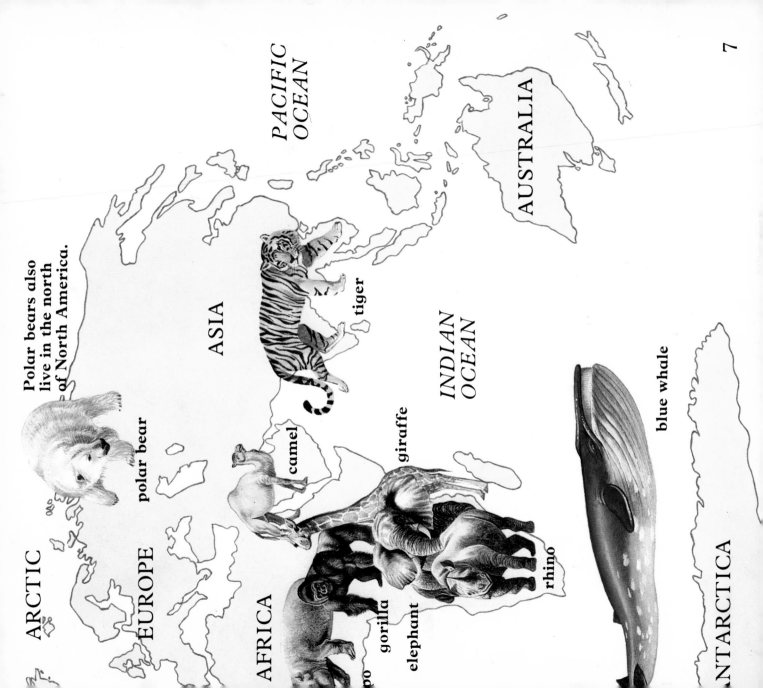

PACIFIC
OCEAN

AUSTRALIA

ASIA

Polar bears also
live in the north
of North America.

tiger

INDIAN
OCEAN

blue whale

ARCTIC

polar bear

EUROPE

camel

giraffe

AFRICA

gorilla

elephant

rhino

NTARCTICA

African elephants are the biggest animals on land. They spend eighteen hours a day feeding because they need so much to eat.

African elephants live in herds. There are female herds and male herds. The elephants bathing at this water hole are females with their calves.

The leader of the herd has spotted danger. She spreads out her ears to make herself look bigger and more frightening. If a dangerous animal gets too close she will charge with a great trumpeting roar.

AFRICAN ELEPHANT
Weighs up to 16,000 pounds. About 12 feet tall. About 20 feet long.
Lives up to 80 years.
Eats leaves, grass, and bark.

Black rhinos live in Africa. They are not really black. They are dark gray and usually covered with mud. They can hear and smell well, but they cannot see very far. Tick birds feed on the ticks and insects that burrow into the rhino's thick skin.

This rhinoceros mother does not see the lioness in the bushes. The tick birds tell her something is wrong by squawking and flapping around her head.

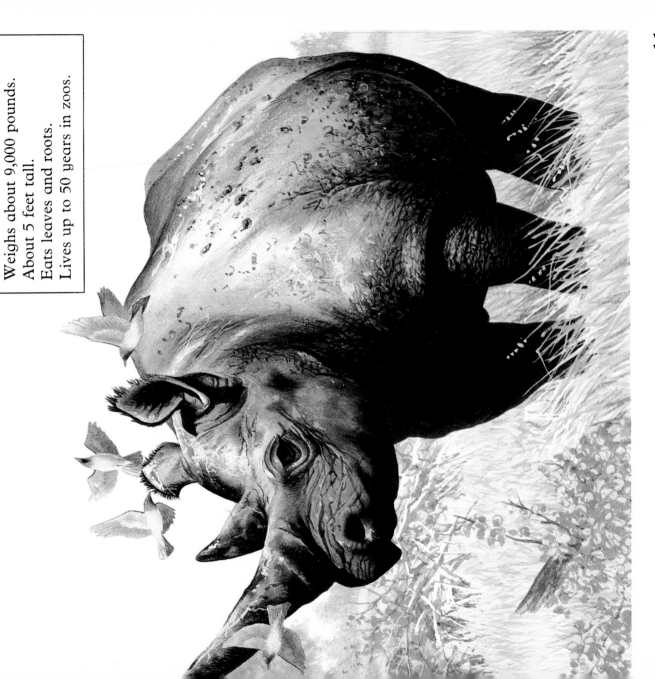

BLACK RHINOCEROS
Weighs about 9,000 pounds.
About 5 feet tall.
Eats leaves and roots.
Lives up to 50 years in zoos.

Hippos spend the daytime in rivers in Africa. It is often difficult to see them because they sink down under the water with just the tops of their heads showing. Sometimes they disappear altogether and walk along the river bottom. Hippos can stay underwater for nearly ten minutes.

In the evening hippos climb up the riverbank and plod off to look for food. They eat grass and other plants and go back to the river the next morning.

HIPPOPOTAMUS
Weighs up to 9,000 pounds.
About 6 feet tall.
About 12 feet long.
Eats mainly grass.

GIRAFFE
Tallest animal in the world; about 18 feet tall.
Babies are 5 feet tall at birth.
Weighs up to 2,800 pounds.
Lives up to 28 years in zoos.
Eats leaves and shoots.
Can gallop at about 28 miles an hour.

Giraffes also live in Africa. This giraffe is eating the leaves of an acacia tree. It avoids the sharp thorns by pulling down a twig with its long tongue. Then the giraffe picks off the leaves with its mouth.

Giraffes do not have to share their food with other animals. Because they are so tall, they can eat leaves and shoots that grow far above the heads of other animals.

Giraffes often feed and rest in clumps of acacia trees. It is difficult to see them among the trees because the squiggles and patches on their skin look like splashes of sunlight and shadow.

GORILLA
Weighs about 550 pounds.
About 5 feet tall.
Eats leaves, shoots, and fruit.

This African gorilla family has found a good place to camp for the night. But the biggest male does not go to sleep. He is keeping watch.

If a leopard or other dangerous animal comes too close, he tries to scare it away. He pulls up clumps of grass and throws them into the air. He hoots and beats his chest. He slaps the ground with his hands and jumps up and down, but it is mostly just an act. Gorillas are very strong, but they are also shy and gentle. They do not fight other animals if they can avoid it.

Many deserts are hot, dry, sandy places.
There is little food or water. Most animals
cannot live in deserts, but camels can.

When a camel drinks, it can fill itself up
with over twenty-six gallons of water. When
a camel eats, some of the food is turned into
fat and stored in its hump. A camel can live
for about fifteen days without eating or
drinking. It just uses up the store of fat in
its hump and the water in its body.

ARABIAN CAMEL
Weighs up to 1,500
pounds.
Up to 7 feet tall.
About 10 feet long.
Lives up to 50 years.
Eats grass and leaves.
Walks at about 3 miles
an hour.

People use camels to help them live in the desert. They use camels to carry things from one place to another. At the end of a long journey a camel is thin and its hump is small and floppy.

Camels do not sink into the sand because they have big padded feet. They have long eyelashes to protect their eyes and can close their nostrils to keep sand from blowing in.

Tigers like to live and hunt on their own. They usually hunt at night because the pattern on their fur makes them difficult to see. In the moonlight the stripes look just like long grass and reeds.

This tiger is creeping up on a marsh deer. When the tiger is close, it rushes forward. With its huge front paws it knocks the deer to the ground and kills it. The tiger eats as much meat as it can. Then it hides the rest to eat another day.

INDIAN TIGER
Biggest cat.
Weighs up to 500 pounds.
About 3 feet tall.
About 10 feet long.
Lives about 20 years.
Eats the meat of deer and pigs; sometimes the meat of buffalo, frogs, rats, and fish.

In this picture it is late summer in North America. The female moose and her calves are eating water lilies. The male moose has waded farther out into the lake. He has huge antlers which he uses in autumn to fight other males. In spring the antlers fall off, and he starts to grow another set. Only the males have antlers.

MOOSE
Biggest deer.
Weighs up to 1,600 pounds.
About 8 feet tall.
Eats water plants, grass, leaves, shoots, and tree bark.
Moose also live in northern parts of Europe, where they are called elk.

In summer, moose eat as much as they can and put on a thick layer of fat. They live off this fat through the winter, when the ground is covered with snow and food is difficult to find.

The two male bison here are battling to find out which is the stronger. They charge each other, clash horns, and push with their huge shoulders. The fight is over when one of them gives up and walks away.

Bison live in herds in North America. In the morning and evening they move slowly over the prairies, eating grass. In the afternoon they lie down and rest. Bison also like dust baths. They roll and rub themselves in the dust and often make hollows in the ground.

NORTH AMERICAN BISON
Weighs up to 3,000 pounds, but females are much lighter than males.
About 7 feet tall.
Stampedes at about 16 miles an hour.

This Arctic polar bear is hunting. It has seen a seal sleeping on the ice and swims slowly toward it. When it is close it leaps onto the ice. Then it kills the seal with one blow from its huge front paw.

Most polar bears spend all year hunting on the ice. But at the beginning of winter pregnant female bears dig dens deep into the snow. They give birth to their cubs in these dens and stay with them all winter. In spring they come out to look for food.

POLAR BEAR

Weighs about 1,100 pounds.

Babies weigh only 2 pounds at birth.

About 5 feet tall.

Lives up to 33 years in zoos.

Eats seals and birds.

Runs at up to 20 miles an hour.

Elephant seals live in South America. These two male elephant seals are fighting. They bellow and roar through their trunklike noses and hurl themselves at each other. When their bodies smack together they look like two giant quivering jellies.

The winner of this battle takes control of this part of the beach. Later on he will mate with any females lying on it and be the father of their pups.

ELEPHANT SEAL
Biggest seal.
Weighs up to 9,000 pounds.
About 20 feet long.
Females are only half as big as this.
Eats squid.
Also known as sea elephant.

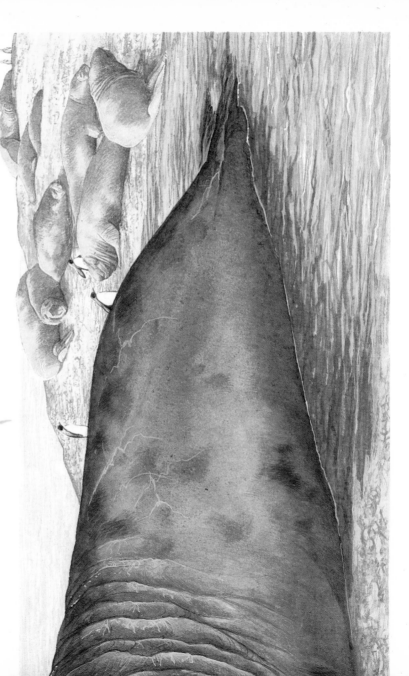

The biggest animals in the world live in the sea. But they are not fishes. They are mammals like all the other animals in this book. They are called blue whales.

Blue whales live mostly in the colder parts of the world's oceans. They are very rare. There are probably only about two thousand of them left in the world.

You can see how huge blue whales are from this picture. They can weigh more than fifteen African elephants.

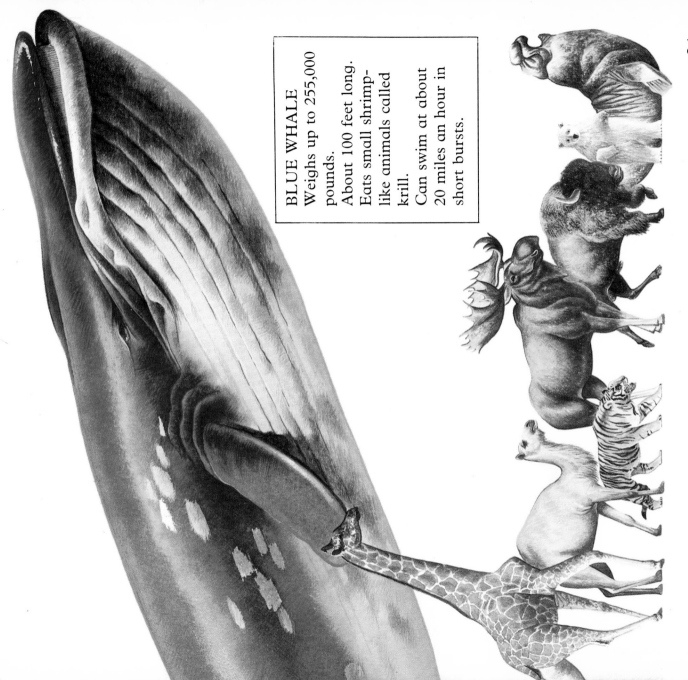

BLUE WHALE
Weighs up to 255,000 pounds.
About 100 feet long.
Eats small shrimp-like animals called krill.
Can swim at about 20 miles an hour in short bursts.

Index

Where to see big animals

You can see big animals in zoos and wildlife parks. To find out if there is one near you:

1 Look up **zoo** in the telephone directory.
2 Ask at the library.
3 Look through the advertisements in a local newspaper.